Tudor Rich and Poor

Haydn Middleton

www.heinemann.co.uk/library
Visit our website to find out more information about **Heinemann Library** books.

To order:
 Phone 44 (0) 1865 888066
 Send a fax to 44 (0) 1865 314091
 Visit the Heinemann Bookshop at www.heinemann.co.uk/library to browse our catalogue and order online.

First published in Great Britain by Heinemann Library, Halley Court, Jordan Hill, Oxford OX2 8EJ, part of Harcourt Education.

Heinemann is a registered trademark of Harcourt Education Ltd.

Editorial: Lucy Thunder and Helen Cox
Design: Jo Hinton-Malivoire, Richard Parker and Tinstar Design Limited (www.tinstar.co.uk)
Illustrations: Tokay Interactive Ltd
Picture Research: Rebecca Sodergren
Production: Séverine Ribierre

Originated by Ambassador Litho Ltd
Printed in China

ISBN 0 431 14619 5 (hardback)
07 06 05 04 03
10 9 8 7 6 5 4 3 2 1

ISBN 0 431 14629 2 (paperback)
08 07 06 05 04
10 9 8 7 6 5 4 3 2 1

British Library Cataloguing in Publication Data
Middleton, Haydn
Tudor Rich and Poor. – (People in the past)
305.5'234'0942'09031
A full catalogue record for this book is available from the British Library.

Acknowledgements
The publishers would like to thank the following for permission to reproduce photographs:

AKG p**9**; Art Archive p**22**; Ashmolean museum p**10**; Bridgeman Art Archive pp**16**, **17**, **19**, **21**, **24**, **30**, **43**; Chris Honeywell p**20**; Collections pp**13** (Paul Watts), **23** (John Miller); **38** (Robert Hallmann); The College of Arms p**18**; Coventry Tourist Board p**33**; Fotomas Index pp**7**, **8**, **15**, **37**; Haydn Middleton p**36**; Historic Royal Palaces p**11**; Hulton Getty pp**27**, **41**; Mansell Collection p**25**; Mary Evans Picture Library pp**6**, **28**; National Portrait Gallery p**42**; Osie Palmer p**31**.

Cover photograph of the Supper at Emmaus, 16th century, reproduced with permission of Bridgeman Art Library.

The publishers would like to thank Rebecca Vickers for her assistance with the preparation of this book.

Every effort has been made to contact copyright holders of any material reproduced in this book. Any omissions will be rectified in subsequent printings if notice is given to the publishers.

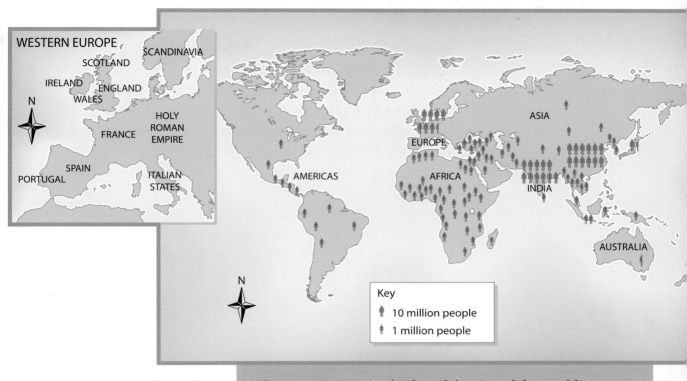

This map gives a rough idea of the size of the world's **population** in early Tudor times. There were far more people living in Euope and Asia than in the rest of the world, and hardly any in America. Europe was split into different countries, some of which are shown here.

As you will find in this book, we know far more about the rich in Tudor times than the poor, since more records about them have survived. However, we can use lots of clues to find out how the poor lived too.

Tudor money note

In this book, Tudor sums of money are shown in pounds (£), shillings (s) and pennies (d). There were 12d in a shilling and 20s in a pound – which was worth a lot more then! Most people earned less than £10 in a whole year, and you could go to the theatre for a single penny.

Four sorts of people

'We in England divide our people commonly into four sorts – gentlemen, citizens, **yeomen**, and labourers. First there are the gentlemen. After the King, the chief gentlemen are the prince, dukes, marquises, earls, viscounts and barons. These are called … lords and **noblemen**. Next are knights, esquires, and last of all those who are simply called gentlemen.'

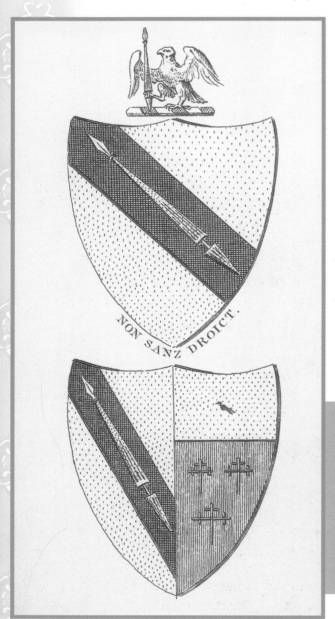

NON SANZ DROICT.

Those words come from the book *Description of England*, written in 1577 by a church minister called William Harrison. He then described the other three sorts of people. Citizens came next – they lived in cities and did important jobs there. Third came the 'yeomen', who owned a certain amount of land and were quite well off. The fourth and last sorts of people were labourers and craftspeople – poor farm-workers, tailors, shoemakers, carpenters, bricklayers and so on. 'As for slaves,' Harrison added proudly, 'we have none' (for there *were* slaves in some other countries).

The coat of arms or badge granted to John Shakespeare when he became a gentleman in 1596. Featuring a falcon and a spear, it was covered almost entirely with gold and silver. Ordinary colours would have been cheaper but less impressive. The whole Shakespeare family, including John's famous writer son William, became 'gentle' at the same time.

Among the fourth sort

The last and poorest of Harrison's groups was easily the largest. The poor had no say or power and were there to be ruled over. Richer people

A Tudor street scene showing some of the people who belonged to Harrison's 'fourth sort' – the poor. Most Tudor artists created pictures of rich people only.

usually looked down on them, feeling 'superior' to them in every way. They sometimes called poor folk 'proles' from an old Latin word. It means they served their country not by creating wealth, but only by producing children.

Yet it is not always clear *how* rich or poor Tudor people were. Townspeople outside London, for example, might complain about how poor they were – but this was often just to avoid paying large amounts of **tax**. Some Tudor poor people got rich and rose up in society. Meanwhile some rich people found themselves struggling for money and fell down in society.

Going up in the world

Men rising up the social ladder wanted other people to know about their success. So they applied to become a 'gentleman'. This allowed them to display a 'coat of arms' (see picture on the left). It could be painted, embroidered or carved on a man's furniture, windows or even worn on his clothing. It was an expensive business. A certificate or 'patent' of gentility could cost £100, plus all the expenses needed to display the coat of arms. In 1596 John Shakespeare, a glove-maker in Stratford-upon-Avon, was made a gentleman in this way. By comparison, the fine house into which he then moved his family may have cost only £60.

Knowing your place

In Tudor times, a small number of people owned most of the country's wealth. The poor heavily outnumbered the rich, and often led terribly hard lives. Yet they very rarely worked together to try to get a fairer deal for themselves. Why was this?

Chains and bodies

Today both rich and poor people can vote in elections. By voting they decide who governs the country. They also make sure that their own voices are heard. This did not happen in Tudor times. Most people were expected simply to get on with their work and obey their 'superiors'. They were definitely not expected to rebel.

The most important superior of all was God. Tudors believed that God had created a 'Great Chain'. It stretched from God himself right down to lifeless objects. In this Chain, everyone and everything had a fixed place. Kings were higher than church officials and gentlemen, who were higher than poor farmers or labourers, and they in turn were higher than animals, plants and stones. God would be displeased if the chain was ever broken. So if poor people rebelled, they could expect terrible suffering in their life and the **afterlife**.

This crowd at St. Paul's Cross in London is listening to a sermon. Priests made it clear to the rich and poor alike that, 'Almighty God has created and arranged all things in heaven, earth and waters, in a most excellent and perfect order.'

A German picture from 1532, showing **peasants** at the bottom of a 'social tree', with their 'superiors' on the branches above them. This artist clearly had his own ideas, for peasants are at the top here, too!

Some government writers put this another way. They claimed that all England's people fitted together like different parts of a body. Some of the jobs were less enjoyable than others, but all were essential. A kingdom (or body) ran smoothly only if all its people (or parts) worked properly.

According to one Tudor bishop, the main reason why people 'behaved themselves' was because they were so afraid of being punished by God. This also helps to explain why the poor put up with such hard living conditions. On pages 40–41 you can find out what happened when they did not.

The sermon of obedience

People were supposed to take great notice of what priests told them in church. So the government made sure priests read out special **sermons**, explaining why 'superiors' should be obeyed. 'Every kind of person has a duty and a rank,' said one sermon. 'If you take away Kings, Princes, rulers, judges and others, no man will ride along the highway unrobbed. No man will sleep in his own bed unkilled. No man will keep his wife, children and belongings … And there will follow all sorts of trouble, and the utter destruction of souls, bodies, goods and the country.'

Homes of the rich

Rich Tudor people liked to show off their wealth by building beautiful houses or extending them. In earlier Tudor times, no one spent more on his homes than King Henry VIII. Today his brick-built palace at Hampton Court still stands in its splendid gardens in Surrey. He received it as a present from Cardinal Thomas Wolsey. There was space inside for Wolsey's household of over 500 people, with 280 rooms for guests. The king made it even larger. When he held court there, around 1000 people might be staying.

Building boom

'The houses of the **nobility** are made of brick and hard stone,' wrote William Harrison in 1577. 'They are so magnificent and stately, that even the most ordinary house of a **baron** nowadays often matches that of a prince in olden times. If ever excellent building flourished in England, it is now.'

During Elizabeth I's reign, there was a craze for new building and home improvement among the nobility. Wealthy **merchants**, country gentlemen and successful farmers joined in the building spree. Glass had become cheaper and more plentiful. Windows grew to such a size and number that a house like Hardwick Hall, in Derbyshire, was said to have 'more glass than wall'.

This sketch of Hampton Court Palace dates from 1558. Its site was chosen as the 'most healthy spot within 20 miles of London'. The city could easily be reached by barge on the river Thames, which is shown in the foreground.

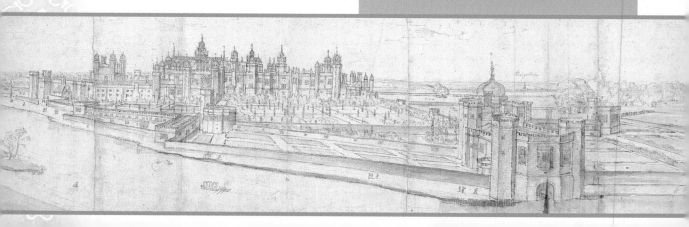

On his travels around the kingdom, Harrison noted 'a multitude of chimneys lately erected' – like these ones, which have survived at Hampton Court. Many large houses had fireplaces in smaller, individual rooms. These 'withdrawing chambers' gave some privacy in busy households.

In the greatest noble houses, the lord and lady ate in the lavishly decorated 'great chamber', received visitors there, and watched plays and **masques**. There might also be a 'long gallery', used to display paintings. People would walk up and down the gallery to get some indoor exercise. Grand houses had to be large and luxurious enough to entertain a **monarch** on a visit. Yet they had none of the basic home comforts we expect today – such as running water, electric lighting and central heating.

Nonsuch Palace

Henry VIII's most ambitious building project was Nonsuch Palace. Begun in 1538, it stood six miles south-east of Hampton Court. A whole village had to be destroyed to make room for all the king's builders and craftspeople. It had two courtyards, with two magnificent eight-sided towers at either end of its southern **façade**. The grounds included a fountain, a maze and 200 pear trees. By the time Henry died in 1547, it had cost £24,000, but was still not finished. Elizabeth I often held court there, but a century after she died it had been knocked down.

Home improvements

When someone died in Tudor times, a list of his or her possessions was made. This list was called an **inventory**. By looking at surviving inventories – usually of well-off people – we can try to work out what the insides of homes were like. We can also tell what Tudor people owned by studying the wills they made. These were documents in which they left or 'willed' their things to relatives or friends. People still make wills today.

John Lawson, quite a wealthy man, was living in the city of Chester in 1580. His inventory lists the possessions in his house and what they were worth. Some of the items were:

'In the hall one iron fireplace, with all the parts belonging to it, 6s 8d. A drawing table with a carpet on it, a bench, and three buffet stools, 13s 4d … One cupboard, with a Danish chest and one pair of tables 18s. Eleven cushions 4s. One dagger with a hanger 5s … In the inner chamber one servant's bed, two covers, one pair of sheets and one **bolster** 5s. One cupboard 5s. Eighteen pieces of **pewter** such as plates and dishes, one basin, four saucers, one **chamber pot**, one quart pot, two short wide pots, one pint pot and two salt cellars 20s …'

The farmer's widow

An inventory from 1531 lets us glimpse the contents of a Devon farmhouse. A widow called Katherine Robbyns lived there. She was not an especially rich woman, but her kitchen still included a **range**, pans, pots, brass and earthenware bowls, plus casks, crocks and sieves for brewing beer and 'a pipe and three little casks to put it in'. There was also a 'distaff' stick that she used for her spinning, with three pounds of yarn and eleven pounds of wool. Outside, she kept all her animals, including an ox, three cows, a horse, a pig and thirteen sheep.

This cottage was built early in the 16th century. We can check from inventories what sort of furniture people had and recreate the insides of Tudor homes.

Changing rooms

In southern England especially, the insides of Tudor homes like John Lawson's were changing fast. New large glass windows were letting more light into rooms. Therefore people with money were buying furniture that looked attractive, as well as being useful.

Rich people's sitting rooms, which they called parlours, were finely decorated, too. They had carved wooden panels on the walls, plaster patterns on the ceiling, even colourful coats of arms in the windows. Meanwhile on the floor, rushes might be scattered in winter, then sweet smelling herbs and flowers in the summer.

Even slightly less wealthy people were taking more care over interior decoration. Their sturdy wooden beds were covered with decoratively stitched tapestries or silk hangings. They displayed carpets from places like Turkey on their tables. Then at mealtimes, instead of using old-fashioned wooden spoons and plates, they might have bought pewter or silver versions, which looked much more impressive.

Dressing up

Most fabrics do not survive for centuries, so clothes usually rot away. To find out what smart Tudor outfits were like, we can look at paintings from the time or read descriptions and **inventories**. One description tells us that Queen Elizabeth I collected wardrobes full of dresses. Many were encrusted with precious stones. Then she dazzled her **subjects** into obedience with outfits like her white silk gown 'bordered with pearls the size of beans.'

Only the rich could afford to dress fashionably. There were no glossy magazines to tell men and women about what wealthy European people were wearing. By 1600, however, small dolls dressed in the latest French fashions were being sent from Paris.

Lace collars, silk shoes

Fashionable late-Tudor clothes were expensive but impractical. Men's starched collars called 'ruffs' could be more than 30 centimetres wide! According to the **Puritan** writer Philip Stubbes, 'they go flip-flap in the wind and lie upon their shoulders like a dishcloth.' Men's hats were popular, looking at times like church steeples 'standing a quarter of a yard above the crown of their heads.' Rich women wore frames called 'farthingales' under embroidered gowns to make their skirts stand out. Some dresses had cuts and slashes made in them to show different colours and types of material beneath. Shoes of velvet, silk or soft leather looked pretty, but were hardly made to last.

Puritan disapproval

Philip Stubbes was a writer and a Puritan at the end of Tudor times. He believed that God preferred people to wear plain, simple clothing. Yet the rich dressed up like peacocks, and carried little mirrors around to admire themselves in. 'Some women are even not content with their own hair,' Stubbes wrote about wigs. 'They buy other hair, either from horses, mares, or any other strange beasts, and dye it.' It is unlikely however that many rich Tudor women wore wigs, unless they lost their own hair in old age.

Dress codes

Another way to find out what people wore is to study 'Sumptuary Laws' passed by Tudor governments. These were laws saying what Tudor people could wear. This comes from 1559: 'No one shall wear any silk in hat, bonnet, nightcap, girdle, **scabbard**, **hose**, shoes or spur leathers except the son and heir or the daughter of a knight, or the knight's wife, or a man who is worth £200 in goods.' The government hoped in this way to keep people in their 'proper' places. Yet many rising Tudor people ignored the laws. 'There is now such a mingle-mangle of dress,' complained one writer in 1585, 'that it is very hard to know who is **noble**, who is a gentleman and who is not.'

This painting, from 1600, shows quite wealthy people gathered together for a feast next to the River Thames near London. By studying pictures like this, we can learn what clothes the Tudors wore. This was a special occasion, for which the people dressed up. They probably wore much simpler clothes when they were not out in public.

Food of the rich

Elizabethan nobles spent huge amounts of money on buildings, clothes, funerals and tombs. They saw no point in hiding their wealth. They also used their riches to provide lavish supplies of food and drink for their guests (and for themselves).

William Harrison wrote in 1577 that, 'No day passes without them having not only beef, mutton, veal, lamb, kid, pork, rabbit, **capon** – or whatever of these is in season – but also some portion of red or fallow deer, beside great variety of fish and wild fowl and various other delicacies.' The diners ate only a little of each dish. Then they sent the leftovers back to the kitchen, where the servants would have found a use for them!

Fish days

Tudor farm animals were leaner than today's beasts, so their meat had less fat. Rich people ate few vegetables with their meat – vegetables were seen as poor people's food. On Fridays, Saturdays and for the 40 days before Easter, however, it was against the law to eat meat. On these days the rich ate fish instead. This was once a religious custom. It became a way for the government to support the kingdom's fishermen and fishmongers.

This portrait shows Lord Cobham's family. Children and adults ate and drank the same things – even the beer and wine. A book of table manners from 1577 told children to 'pick not thy teeth with thy knife nor … foul not the place with spitting where thou do sit.'

No fridges

Since they had no fridges, Tudor people ate a lot of fresh food. Most apples, pears, plums and cherries were eaten soon after being picked in the autumn. Some were preserved in syrup to last over the winter. Many farm animals, too, were slaughtered for meat in the autumn. This saved the expense of feeding them through the winter. Some of the meat was preserved by rubbing it with salt. Later it was cooked with powerful spices from abroad to improve its taste.

Sweet-toothed Tudors

Rich Tudors loved sugary foods, and foreign visitors remarked on the bad effect on their teeth. After their meat or fish courses, they devoured sweets made from 'marchpane' or marzipan – a mixture of ground almonds, sugar and rose water, coloured with vegetable dyes then shaped into models of ships, castles, fruits, flowers or animals.

A wealthy Tudor home. The kitchen staff are serving dinner to the family in the next room.

The rich at play

The Tudor rich had plenty of time to enjoy themselves. Back in the **Middle Ages**, the king's wealthiest **subjects** had to fight for him in wars. By Tudor times, paid soldiers did most of the fighting. The rich still took part in **jousting** (see picture). They also took great pleasure in hunting deer, boars, foxes, hares and even badgers.

In earlier Tudor times, **nobles** and gentlemen took great pride in creating deer parks for hunting in. In the 1530s, the travel writer John Leland counted fifteen big deer parks in Leicestershire alone. Rich men were also expected to spend money as **patrons**. They supported poor but gifted artists, writers, actors, musicians or builders, hoping to share in the glory of their great creations.

Court entertainment

Most of the kingdom's richest people spent some time having fun at court. Court was wherever the **monarch** happened to be. Queen Elizabeth moved constantly from royal palace to palace, and in summer she 'progressed' around the countryside, staying at the homes of her wealthiest subjects. These subjects were expected not just to feed and give rooms to the Queen's large travelling party. They also had to lay on **masques**, parties and **pageants**.

King Henry VIII – also a fine tennis player – jousting in front of his first wife, Catherine of Aragon. Some tournaments ended in tragedy. In 1559 King Henry II of France was wounded in the eye by a **lance**, and died days later.

This painting by Nicholas Hilliard shows Elizabeth I playing a **lute**.

Surviving records show what kinds of entertainers appeared at court, and how much they were paid. During the Christmas period of 1579–80, plays were put on by travelling theatre groups and another by 'the children of Her Majesty's Chapel'. There was also a **bear-baiting** performance, and a show put on by acrobats. The Queen must have enjoyed the acrobatics, since she paid them their fee of £6 13s 4d plus an extra £3 6s 8d as a personal 'tip'.

A royal musician

Some rich Tudor people learned to play musical instruments for fun. In 1564 Sir James Melville visited Elizabeth I's court. 'My Lord of Hunsdon led me up to a quiet gallery,' he wrote later, 'where I might hear the Queen play upon the **virginals** … I pulled aside the tapestry that hung before the door of the chamber. Then I went inside and heard her play excellently well. She stopped as soon as she turned and saw me, and came forward – seeming to strike me with her left hand. She said that she played only when she was alone and sad, and never in front of men.'

A courtier's wife in the country

Young unmarried Tudor **noblewomen** passed a lot of time at court. After they married, many spent their lives in country houses. Meanwhile their husbands served the **monarch** at court and came home whenever they could. Some noble wives ran their husbands' **estates** for them. Others, like Lady Grace Mildmay, simply supervised a large staff of servants. Lady Grace, whose home was at Apethorpe in Northamptonshire, wrote an **autobiography** that clearly shows us how rich Tudor women lived.

In 1621, a year after Lady Grace Mildmay's death, her daughter Jane set up this tomb to her mother and father. Lady Grace's autobiography shows that she had little to do with Jane's upbringing.

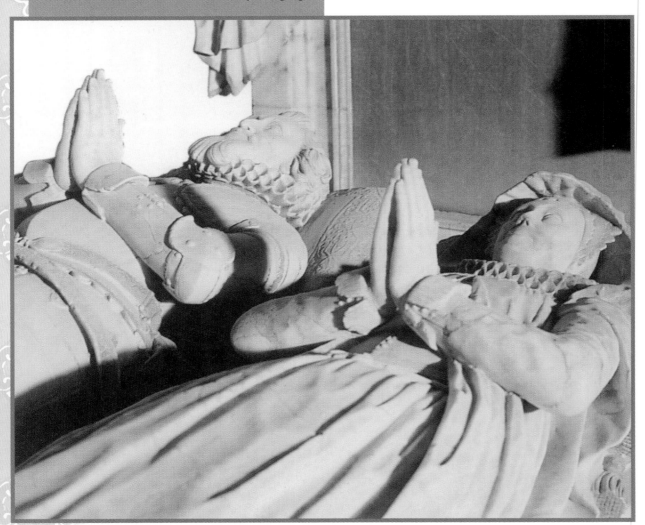

A distant relationship

Lady Grace's husband was Sir Anthony Mildmay. Their marriage was arranged when she was 14 years old and Anthony was about 20. Like his father Sir Walter, who also lived at Apethorpe, Anthony was an important member of the ruling class. Anthony had to spend a lot of time away from home, serving Queen Elizabeth I at court or as an **ambassador** abroad. Grace saw little of him, and they had only one child – Jane, born in 1582.

Work and pastimes

Grace was seldom idle. Like other women in her position, she enjoyed reading the Bible, praying, playing the **lute** and needlework. Another interest of hers was studying health matters. She made medicines in large quantities, discussed cures with several doctors, and helped sick people who came to her from nearby. When she died in 1620, she left money to pay someone to teach the local children to read and write.

While Grace was alive, her main 'job' was to run the Mildmay home. For this, she relied on plenty of servants. She described them in this way:

'Of the three maids one is for cooking, one is for tending poultry and making butter, cheese and necessaries, the third serves as a chambermaid … Of the men servants, one is to bake and brew, one is to cultivate the soil and provide beef and mutton and serve as a **caterer**. Two are personal servants … One looks after the horse. One serves as a caterer when the other servant is away on other duties. Lastly there is a **footboy**.'

Mildmay medicine

This was one of the many cures recorded by Lady Grace. It was for people who suffered from 'falling sickness' or **epilepsy**. 'Take an old toad and slay it, then split him and take out all his insides except his liver… Wash it very clean, and lay it on a tile stone in an oven after the bread is taken out. Then dry it and make a powder from it and mix it with a small amount of cinnamon, and give a hazelnut shell full of it to the patient washed down with some ale or beer.'

The London rich

London, England's capital city, was the centre of Tudor government. It was also the centre for the law courts, trade, banking and fashion. By 1600 nearly 200,000 people lived there – 10 times more than in Norwich, England's second-biggest city. Among them were many wealthy people. Among the wealthiest were **merchants** who made their fortunes in trading – like Sir John Spencer. When he died in 1610, he was worth at least £300,000. That almost certainly made him England's richest man.

In the city

Most rich Londoners lived in the central parts of the city. Many merchants carried out their business from their homes, which stood on narrow, badly paved, unclean streets. Land to build on cost so much that they might have only dark little rooms on the ground floor. They could, however, expand their mainly wooden homes upstairs, and let the upper storeys overhang the roadway. In these cramped conditions, fatal diseases often spread – including the dreaded plague.

This is a map of London from around 1560. The city's street-plan today is still very similar. The four people at the front could be called typical rich Tudor Londoners: a wealthy merchant and his wife, accompanied by an armed attendant and a plainly dressed servant woman.

The Staple Inn Houses, built in 1586, still stand in London's High Holborn today. Much of old London was destroyed in the Great Fire of 1666.

Rich Londoners could afford to pay the fees demanded by doctors (sometimes as high as £1 per day). But when plagues broke out, doctors could do little except try to stop them from spreading. In a single outbreak in 1563, one person out of every four or five died in the capital city.

In mid-Tudor times there were plenty of open spaces for the rich to enjoy, just a short distance from the city centre. Hog Lane, which ran from Whitechapel to Spitalfields, 'had on both sides fair hedgerows of elm trees, with bridges and easy stiles to pass over into the pleasant fields. Here citizens could walk, shoot and refresh their dulled spirits in the sweet and wholesome air' (from John Stow's *Survey of London*, 1598).

Tudor transport

Rich Londoners had a choice of ways to get around their city. They could travel by barge on the river Thames, which was London's busiest 'road' of all. Or they could travel in uncomfortable, windowless horse-drawn coaches and carriages. As John Stow noted in his *Survey*, these added to London's traffic problems. 'The growing number of carriages … and coaches in the narrow streets and lanes is dangerous, as daily experience proves. The coachman rides behind the horse tails, lashes them and does not look behind him … By law the leading horse of every carriage should be led by hand, but this does not happen.'

Rich and poor at London's fair

Rich people were never far away from the poor in Tudor London. Even in the city's 'posh' central **parishes**, poor people might live in shacks behind rich **merchants**' houses. Rich and poor also mingled on the streets. They even enjoyed their entertainment together – at theatres like The Globe just south of the River Thames, and especially at the great fairs.

Tudor fairs were different from the modern sort. All kinds of people went to them – to look for jobs or workers, to buy and sell goods, to watch sportsmen and actors perform, and to eat, drink and gamble. Usually these great fairs were held during the summer and early autumn. The greatest in England were held at Stourbridge, near Cambridge and at Smithfield, just to the north-west of London's city walls. This one was called Bartholomew Fair, and people travelled to it from far and wide.

In Tudor times crowds were less common than today. There were far fewer people and towns were much smaller. People did get together regularly at church services, but in most parishes, less than 100 worshippers gathered each week. Outside London, the biggest crowds were at feast days, great weddings, markets and fairs.

Gingerbread, pork and pie powder

At Bartholomew Fair you could refresh yourself with gingerbread dolls called 'Bartholomew babies', or delicious roast pork at the stall of Ursula the Pig Woman. At different times plenty of 'monsters' were on show: dancing dogs, 'a goose with three legs', and a trained monkey that jumped over a chain whenever it heard the name of an English **monarch**, but stayed still when he heard the name of the King of Spain or the **Catholic Pope**!

Stewards tried to make sure there was no violence at the Fair, and that the food and drink on sale were of high quality. If anyone was caught stealing, he or she could be dealt with at a special Fair law court, called a Court of Pie Powder. This court could punish dishonest traders as well.

One of the wonders performed at Bartholomew Fair – showing how the head of John the Baptist was 'cut off' in front of gasping spectators.

Fun at the Fair

Londoners of all sorts went to Bartholomew Fair. 'At each Fair's opening in August,' wrote German visitor Paul Hentzner in 1598, 'it is usual for the mayor, attended by the twelve principal **aldermen**, to walk in a neighbouring field … When they arrive at a place where a tent is pitched, the mob begins to wrestle before them, two at a time. Each winner receives a prize. Then live rabbits are turned loose among the crowd. They are pursued by a number of boys, who try to catch them, with all the noise they can make.' While Hentzner watched all this, one of his companions had his purse stolen!

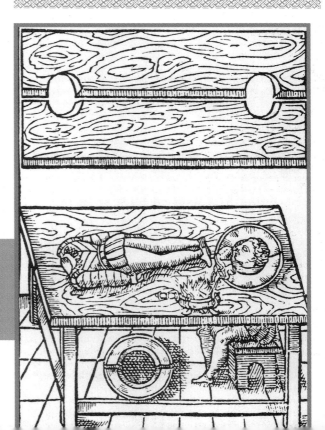

The London poor

To many poor people living elsewhere in England, London sounded like a place to get rich quick. About 6000 of them arrived in the city each year, hoping to make better lives for themselves. Some succeeded, but many found no work to do nor homes to live in. The unluckiest ones slipped into a dangerous London 'underworld' of beggars, part-time entertainers and criminals.

Struggling to survive

Many poor people worked at home as poorly paid craftspeople or labourers. Men of the same trade or craft tended to live in the same areas – street names like Ironmongers Lane, **Hosier** Lane and **Bowyers** Row show what kind of work used to be done there. Compared to today, their living conditions were awful. Without piped water or their own supply, they relied on door-to-door carriers who sold water from pumps and wells. They had to make do without baths or lavatories.

Many poor people often went hungry, too. Poor city families were less able to grow their own food than those living in the country were. They depended on a cheap supply of daily bread, but after bad harvests, food grew scarce and cost more than they could afford. During the 1550s food and fuel prices rose by nearly 50 per cent.

Sad ends

These entries come from a London **parish** register of burials, 1593–98. They show what desperate lives some poor Londoners led, before dying homeless on the streets:

'Edward Ellis, a vagrant, who died in the street …
A cripple that died in the street before John Awsten's door …
Margaret, a deaf woman, who died in the street.
A young man vagrant having no home who died in the street before the door of Joseph Hayes … He was about eighteen years old. I could not learn his name.'

Then between 1594 and 1597 the price of flour almost tripled. For families who only just earned enough to buy their daily bread already, it was hard to cope.

In early Tudor times, richer Londoners gave handouts to poor and jobless people who could not help themselves. By 1547 not enough money was being raised in this way, so the city officials made payments compulsory (required by law). Local 'poor relief' schemes like this were later turned into laws by Parliament, and richer people all over the kingdom had to obey them.

Mary Frith, the daughter of a London shoemaker, dressed up as a man and became one of the many criminals on the city's streets. She was nicknamed 'Moll Cutpurse'.

On the road

'The most dangerous people are the wandering soldiers and other stout rogues of England. There are three or four hundred of these idle people in each county – they travel in twos and threes to beg.'

A **Justice of the Peace** in Somerset wrote that in 1596. England's rulers fiercely disapproved of travelling beggars or vagrants (which just means wanderers). They preferred poor people to stay in one place, where they could be supervized. People on the move seemed threatening – especially if they were armed ex-soldiers or sailors home from the wars. At the very least, people thought they might use their weapons to threaten and rob people.

'Stout rogues'

England's rulers also disapproved of what they called 'stout rogues'. These were beggars who were really quite capable of working. Sometimes they pretended to be ill or injured, just to get richer people to take pity on them and give them handouts.

A vagrant is whipped through a town's streets. This man may genuinely have been looking for work, but until 1576, the Tudor government did not accept that some men could not help being unemployed. Only after 1576 did it start to try to help them.

SPECTATUM ADMISSI RI TENEATIS IMICA

Other types of people who took to the roads – travelling musicians called minstrels, travelling salesmen, or pedlars and families looking for work – were feared and suspected, too. William Harrison guessed there were 10,000 vagrants in England in 1577. Fairly or unfairly, they were all seen as lazy, dishonest and a major threat to public order if they banded together.

The government's harsh response

How would you like to be whipped, and have a hole burned through your ear – just because you had been caught on the roads looking for a job? If you were over fourteen years of age in 1572, this could have happened to you by law. At least it was less brutal than an earlier, cancelled law of 1547. That made it possible for vagrants to be turned into slaves for the rest of their lives.

By the end of Tudor times, the government was beginning to see that not all vagrants deserved punishment. By a series of Poor Laws starting in 1576, people who avoided work and begged instead could still be whipped and sent back to the county they last lived in. If they kept getting caught, they could be sent to work in overseas **colonies**. Work was also to be found, however, for those who were truly seeking jobs.

Work for those who want it

In Tudor times there was not enough work for everyone to do. From 1576, Tudor 'Poor Laws' helped solve the problem by creating jobs: 'So that young people may not become idle rogues, and so that those who are rogues at the present may not have any excuse that they cannot get work, and so that any who is poor and needy can have work, we order the setting up of a store of wool or other stuff to work with in all cities and towns. This can be given to those who say they have no work.'

The 'deserving poor'

Some rich Tudors knew that not all poor people were simply lazy. They understood that the very old, the very young and the very sick had no way of earning money for themselves. Such people were known as the 'deserving poor' – meaning that they deserved to be helped out a little. Local officials gave them permits or licences to beg in certain places. Meanwhile, other rich people – especially **merchants** – helped with handouts called **alms**. These might be gifts of money to buy food with, or even places for the homeless to live in. Before he died in 1529, Devon merchant John Greneway made these arrangements in his will:

'I, John Greneway, a merchant of Tiverton in the county of Devon, have founded an **almshouse** in the town … for five poor men to live in … every one to have rooms for himself. And every one of them shall receive 8 pence a week, for ever, to pray daily for me, for Joan my wife, and for all Christian people.'

From rich to poor, by law

From 1563, Tudor governments made the rich help the poor by law. People had to pay a regular 'rate' – an amount of money that depended on how well-off they were.

This Dutch painting from around 1600 shows bread being given to 'the deserving poor'. Without charity like this from richer people, life would have been very much harder for the poor people of Europe.

The box below shows how much money was raised in a typical **parish** and how it was spent. By 1601 local officials called **overseers** were organizing all the care for England's poor. Their work included working out what 'poor rates' people should pay, and making sure the money came in. Yet the sums they raised were small compared to the help given by people like John Greneway. In ten counties in Elizabeth's reign only £12,000 came from local rates. The amount that came from private charity was £174,000.

This almshouse was provided by Tudor merchant John Greneway in the town of Tiverton, Devon. The poor men given homes there had to pray for the generous merchant in its small chapel. 'Rest a while ye that may: Pray for me by night and day,' is carved on the outside wall.

How the money was spent

Parish records show how much money was raised in poor rates and how it was spent. In a district of Norwich, surviving accounts from 1598–99 show that £110 4s and 4d was collected. The money was spent in a variety of ways: £2 7s 3d was paid 'to the extremely sick'; 1s 8d was paid 'for nursing a young infant left in the parish one week'; 9s 1d went to making a boy called Thomas Clarke an **apprentice**, and £1 13s 8d was used to pay 'for caring for a poisoned man'. But the biggest sum of £24 8s was paid to parish overseers for collecting the cash.

Poor possessions

There were huge numbers of poor people in Tudor England. In the 1520s, over 25 per cent of the population was too poor to be asked to pay **taxes**. It is hard for us today to imagine how few things such people owned. When the very poor died, they left no wills. We cannot tell from **inventories** what possessions they had, but the wills of labourers and poor townspeople show that even they had only the bare necessities. In 1592 a poor carpenter in Rye, Sussex, left just his tools, a cooking pot, two spoons, a knife and a piece of bacon!

The poor also made do with simple home-made woollen clothes. They might own just one set – and wear it until it fell to pieces.

Desperate dwellings

In 1602 the writer Richard Carew described some poor people's cottages in Cornwall. He said that they had: 'Walls of earth, low thatched roofs, few partitions [thin walls], no floorboards or glass windows, and scarcely any chimneys other than a hole in the wall to let out the smoke.' Most poor people's homes were far too flimsy to survive until today. From this description we can imagine how small and draughty they were.

A lucky find

Almost all poor Tudor people's clothes have rotted away now. Some, however, have survived by pure chance. In 1545, for example, a Tudor warship named the *Mary Rose* sank at Portsmouth. Deep mud preserved many of the items on board – including the leather shoes and jackets on the skeletons of ordinary soldiers and sailors. In the late 20th century they were brought up to the surface by divers and put in a special *Mary Rose* museum at Portsmouth.

This is Ford's Hospital almshouse in Coventry as it is today. The poorest people could live here in far greater comfort than in houses they built for themselves.

The poorest of the poor made rough houses called hovels out of mud and branches on heaths and in forests. Many people believed that if squatters built a home on wasteland in one night, the law said they could stay there. People with a little more money used whatever local materials they could afford. In the north of England, stone and clay were common. Cob (clay strengthened with straw) was used in Devon and the Midlands. Most often a wooden frame was put up, then filled with **wattle and daub.**

What did poor people keep inside these dwellings? They had few home comforts. According to William Harrison in his *Description of England* (1577), some might have 'a good round log under their heads instead of a **bolster** or pillow' and no beds but mattresses filled with straw, or 'rough mats covered only with a sheet.'

33

Health and conditions

Most poor people in Tudor times got plenty of fresh air. Those who did farm work got plenty of physical exercise too. In addition, they did not abuse their bodies with cigarettes or other drugs. So were they all very healthy? The answer is no.

The homes of the poor had no **sanitation**. People had to fetch water from wells, springs, local streams or ponds. That meant that washing was very difficult, and people were often dirty – especially if their farm animals shared their living space. In such cramped, unhygienic conditions, germs spread quickly. People did not know that this was how illness and diseases started. When they did fall ill they could not afford to pay doctors to treat them. Instead they relied on medicines made from herbs and plants.

This painting of 'The Harvesters' Meal' by Jan Breughel shows 16th-century people eating heathily on a special occasion. Their normal meals were less satisfying.

Once sick, many people never recovered. In the Devon village of Colyton from 1550 to 1570, for example, roughly one in three children died before they were fifteen years old. During the reign of Elizabeth I, a person could expect to live for just 37 years on average.

Poor diet

One way of building up your body's strength is to eat well. This was often impossible for the Tudor poor. Unlike the rich, they hardly ever ate meat unless they stole rabbits, deer, fish or wild birds. This was called poaching and it could be punished very severely.

Their main food was bread, usually made from barley. The poorest people mixed the barley with flour made from peas, beans or even acorns. They might make a thin porridge from oats, washed down by watered-down beer (but not wine). Labourers' diets also included milk, cheese, lard, plus any vegetables and herbs they grew. Vagrants often had to live off whatever scraps they could pick up on their travels, plus any berries or nuts they found growing wild.

Not to be eaten at home

Many poor people had to go hungry even though they were producing wholesome food. In his book *Poor Husbandman's Advocate*, the writer Richard Baxter explained why. 'If their sow pig or their hens breed, they cannot afford to eat them, but must sell them to pay their rent. They cannot afford to eat the eggs that their hens lay, nor the apples nor the pears that grow on their trees (save some that are rotten) but must make money out of them all. All the best of their butter and cheese they must sell, and feed themselves and their children … with skimmed cheese and skimmed milk and **whey curds**.'

How the poor lived together

Tudor England was divided up into 9000 small areas called **parishes**. In town and country alike, each had its own church and its own priest or 'clergyman'. Parishes differed from place to place, but most of them contained many more poor people than rich. These poor people gathered together in little **communities** that worshipped, worked and played together.

We know a lot about the little community in the Devon parish of Morebath in mid-Tudor times. This is because the local priest, Sir Christopher Trychay, kept detailed records that have survived until today. (He was not a knight. All priests were called 'Sir'.)

The church year

Just 33 families lived in mid-Tudor Morebath. That added up to only about 150 men, women and children tending sheep, growing crops, and making cloth. The people of the parish were named after their farms – like Moore, Timewell, and Wood – or after their jobs, like Smith and Miller. These people were not at all rich, although most were not living 'on the breadline'. They were ordinary poor folk, like thousands more all over the kingdom.

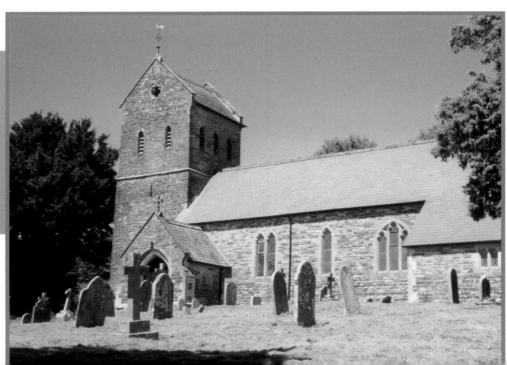

Morebath parish church, which still stands today, although its appearance has changed a little since Tudor times.

Church ales

Next to the parish church in Morebath – as in most parishes – was the church house. This was a kind of Tudor community centre. Visiting **merchants** hired stalls there to sell their goods. Travelling actors performed there and members of the parish and churchwardens also organized banquets called 'church ales' there. Local people were expected to come and buy beer and food, while listening to music made by minstrels. All the money raised was then used for the upkeep of the church and parish.

The people of Morebath followed the same yearly customs as the poor elsewhere. Every spring, for example, people marched around their parishes behind the priest. At special places there were **sermons**, singing and prayers for fine weather and a good harvest that year. There was a lot of eating, drinking and playing around on these holidays. It was the time of year when all arguments or disputes in the community were supposed to be settled.

Christmas was always celebrated for twelve days. During the 40 days leading up to Easter, people were supposed to give up eating meat – no hardship for the poor who hardly ever had meat anyway! Holy days through the year helped to jog people's memories. 'Plant your garlic and beans on St Edmund's Day,' advised one book on farming. It was thought to be unlucky to fit horseshoes on St Loy's Day.

Ploughing was a job for specialists, but all members of the local community helped out at harvest time, including children.

No more monasteries

'Level, level with the ground
The towers do lie,
Which with their golden, glittering tops
Pierced once to the sky.'

That is a verse from a song written in the reign of Queen Elizabeth I. The towers that had fallen in the song belonged to England's 'religious houses'. These were monasteries and nunneries – places where monks, nuns and **friars** had lived and worked for many centuries. Local poor people were supposed to be given any of their leftover food at the gates each day.

The ruins of Castle Acre Priory in Norfolk, a once-thriving monastery closed down by King Henry VIII. Most ex-monks received a little money to live on but had to find new work at a time when jobs were in short supply. Some became priests, some tutors, some **clerks**. There were few jobs for poor, unmarried ex-nuns.

In 1536 there were 825 religious houses, containing nearly 10,000 religious folk, plus thousands more people who worked there. By 1540 there were none – they had all either been sold off, turned to other uses, or become ruined. Why were they all closed down, and what effect did this have?

England breaks with Rome

When Henry VIII became king in 1509, everyone in England was supposed to be a **Catholic** Christian. Everyone, including Henry, had to obey the **Pope** in Rome's religious rules. Around 1530, Henry fell out badly with Pope Clement VII. This was because he was desperate for a son and heir. He wanted to divorce his first wife, Catherine of Aragon, who had not given him a son, and make Anne Boleyn his new queen. The Pope tried to block the divorce. So Henry made himself 'Head of the Church' in England instead, so that he could make his own religious rules.

Free to marry Anne, Henry also decided to shut down the religious houses. He seized the buildings, with all the fine things inside them and the valuable land they stood on. This became known as the '**dissolution** of the monasteries'. Soon he sold lots of them. Rich buyers turned the buildings into grand private homes. Malmesbury Abbey was given to an 'exceeding rich clothier' called William Stump who filled it 'with looms to weave cloth', according to Tudor writer John Leland. Other monasteries became cathedrals, or **parish** churches. Many just fell into ruin as people took the stone and tiles for new buildings.

No more charity?

Many Tudor writers complained after the dissolution of the monasteries. They claimed that the new owners did not give as much to the local poor as the old monks, nuns and friars had. But in some places people had complained before the dissolution too. In 1526, it was said that the monks at St Benet's Holm in Norfolk were feeding their leftover scraps to their dogs, leaving nothing to give away to the poor at the abbey gates. It seems that some monks were better at helping out the needy than others. So it is hard to say exactly how much the dissolution affected England's poor people.

'The many-headed monster'

The Tudor rich worried about the poor. This was partly because they saw the poor's suffering and felt sorry for them. But they were also afraid of them. To the rich, the huge number of poor people in England seemed like a great 'many-headed monster'. Usually this 'monster' was very tame, but what if it suddenly grew violent and attacked the much smaller number of rich people?

It did happen sometimes. Each Tudor **monarch** faced at least one mass protest or rebellion. Ordinary people might form violent crowds because they thought a rich local landowner was treating them badly. Or maybe they disliked new **taxes**, or the latest religious changes. Often it was a mixture of several reasons. In such emergencies, there was no police force or national army to keep order. The government relied mainly on local **nobles** to raise small armies that could break up the crowds.

Sheep and wolves

In times when the rich seemed to be getting richer, some of the poor were bound to feel cheated. In 1549, in the reign of Edward VI, there was a serious rebellion. It was led by a **tanner** and minor landowner called Robert Kett. Some of the poor rebels hated the way rich farmers let their huge flocks of sheep gobble up all the best pasture. In a panic, the government hired German professional soldiers to help destroy the rebel army. About 3000 men were killed.

The constant threat of violence

The government was right to be worried about disorder. Foreign visitors often remarked on how violent ordinary English people could be. Jacob Rathgeb, a German visitor to London, noted in 1592 that 'street boys and **apprentices** collect together in crowds and strike to the right and left unmercifully.' Also, little personal quarrels could quickly turn into full-scale riots. In 1584, a London official reported to Lord Burghley that one Wednesday evening a tailor and a **clerk** had an argument. Soon hundreds of other men had joined in their fight.

The next year, a local poor man claimed that 'as sheep or lambs are a prey to the wolf or lion, so are poor men a prey to rich men.'

Nervous Tudor governments made priests preach **sermons** on the importance of obedience at all times (see page 8). They also took some steps to reduce the suffering of the poor (see page 31). In this way they hoped to stop the 'many-headed monster' from rising up again.

Public executions were supposed to put other people off committing crime or rising in rebellion. Criminals in London were hanged on the **gallows** at Tyburn.

How do we know? – Paintings

What did the Tudor rich and poor actually look like? How exactly did they dress? There was no photography in Tudor times, but we can use paintings from the time to see how the people and their world appeared. The picture below, for example, tells the life story of Tudor **courtier** Sir Henry Unton. It shows him from birth (lower right) to his funeral (middle, under his portrait). In between times it shows him at university and travelling in Italy (both top right), serving the queen as an **ambassador** in France (top middle), going to church and enjoying a banquet.

Detailed portraits like this one do not just show us what individual rich people looked like. They also give us useful clues about how they lived their lives, and even what buildings they lived in.

Sir Henry Unton paid a painter to work on the picture below. Many Tudor **nobles** and gentlemen paid to have simpler portraits painted. The poor could not afford to do this, so we are able to look at far fewer pictures of them today. Painters did however sometimes paint scenes that included 'typical' poor people (see page 30).

This is a painting of Anne of Cleves, who became the fourth wife of King Henry VIII. It was painted by the great German artist Hans Holbein (1497–1543).

When we look at portraits of wealthy Tudors, we have to remember that the artists may be 'bending the truth' a little. (They had to please their **patrons**, or they might not get paid.) Tudor portraits, however – in oils or in water colours – were far more lifelike than paintings from the **Middle Ages**. The rich were so proud of them, they showed them off in 'long galleries' in their homes (see page 11). This gave people in later centuries the idea to show paintings in public art galleries. Today you can visit such galleries all over Britain, and check out the Tudors for yourself!

Image control

Portraits were ordered by Tudor courtiers, **nobles**, gentlemen, **merchants**, the Church, and by the colleges of Oxford and Cambridge Universities. Many of the best were painted by foreigners. Queen Elizabeth I only wanted to see high-quality portraits of herself. From about 1570, all pictures of her had to be based on already existing images or 'patterns', approved by her and her ministers. English painter Nicholas Hilliard (1547–1619) was a favourite artist of the queen. She probably liked the fact that his miniature portraits of her made her look so young!

Timeline

1485	Tudor family begins to rule over England and Wales
1492	Christopher Columbus reaches America
1509–47	Reign of Henry VIII
1529–39	England stops being a Roman **Catholic** country; all the monasteries and nunneries are closed down
1538	**Parish** registers of baptisms, marriages and deaths kept from now on
	Work on Nonsuch Palace is begun
1547	Very harsh law passed against vagrant children
1547–1553	Reign of the boy-king Edward VI
1549	Rebellion in East Anglia led by Robert Kett
1553-58	Reign of Mary I
1558–1603	Reign of Elizabeth I 136 new grammar schools set up
1563	First Tudor Poor Law passed, helping poor families; law also passed setting new rules on **apprenticeship**, wages and work
1564–1616	Life of William Shakespeare
1576	'Poor Law' passed aim to help the poor find work
1577	*Description of England* by William Harrison published
1577–80	Francis Drake becomes first English sea captain to sail around the world
1588	English navy defeats invading Spanish fleet (or Armada)
1601	Most important Poor Law passed
1603	End of Tudor period

Sources and further reading

Sources

The author and Publishers gratefully acknowledge the publications from which sources in the book are drawn. In some cases the wording or sentence structure has been simplified to make the material appropriate for a school readership.

Birth, Marriage and Death, David Cressy (Oxford, 1997)

The Common People: A History from the Norman Conquest to the Present, J. F. C. Harrison (Flamingo, 1984)

Elizabeth I and Her Reign, Ed. Richard Salter (Macmillan Documents and Debates, 1988)

Elizabethan People, Ed. Joel Hurstfield and Alan G.R. Smith (Edward Arnold Documents of Modern History, 1972)

The Elizabethan Underworld, Gamini Salgado (Alan Sutton, 1984)

The Later Tudors, Penry Williams (Oxford, 1995)

Poverty and Vagrancy in Tudor England, John Pound (Longman, 1971)

The Sixteenth Century, Patrick Collinson (Oxford, 2002)

Tudor England, 1485-1603, Ed. Roger Lockyer and Dan O'Sullivan (Longman Sources and Opinions, 1993)

The Tudor Image, Maurice Howard (Tate Gallery, 1995)

The Voices of Morebath, Eamonn Duffy (Yale University Press, 2001)

Further reading

A Tudor Kitchen, Peter Chrisp (Heinemann Library, 1997)

Tudor Children, Jane Shuter (Heinemann Library, 1996)

Tudor Family Life, Jane Shuter (Heinemann Library, 1997)

Life in Tudor Times: Country Life, Jane Shuter (Heinemann Library, 1996)

Websites

www.heinemannexplore.co.uk – contains KS2 History modules including the Tudors.

www.brims.co.uk/tudors/ – information on Tudors for 7–10 year olds.

Glossary

afterlife life after death, something that Tudor people believed in

alderman important local official

alms gift of money to the poor

almshouse house for the poor to live in

ambassador someone representing his king or queen abroad

apprentice young person learning a craft from a master

autobiography person's life story, written by him or herself

baron a type of noble

bear-baiting 'sport' in which dogs were set to attack a chained bear

bolster pillow across a bed

bowyer maker and seller of bows for archery

capon cock bird fattened up for eating

Catholic only Christian faith in western Europe until the 1520s, when people began to follow the new Protestant faith

caterer person who provides meals

chamber pot potty

clerk someone who works in an office

colonies lands taken and ruled over by another country

community group of people living together

cost of living prices that have to be paid for necessary things

courtier person who spent time at a monarch's court as a companion or adviser

dissolution closing down or breaking up of something

Elizabethan during the reign of Queen Elizabeth I (1558–1603)

epilepsy nervous disorder in which the patient has fits

estate person's land and all that stands on it

façade frontage

footboy boy who waited at table and opened doors

friar type of monk who originally begged for a living

gallows simple wooden structure that people were hanged from

hosier dealer in Tudor legwear, known as hose

inventory list of a dead person's possessions

jousting sport in which riders fought on horseback

Justice of the Peace local Tudor official

lance long spear used to fight with when jousting

lute guitar-like musical instrument

masque show featuring drama and music

merchant person who buys and sells goods

Middle Ages centuries before Tudor times

monarch king, queen or other crowned ruler

nobles rich and important men who helped the monarch to run the country. A female noble would be a noblewoman. This class of people were known as the nobility.

Ottoman Turks Turkish people who conquered large parts of eastern Europe and Asia

overseers people in charge

pageant procession, to entertain people

parish local area with its own church and own church official

patron someone who supports and encourages a creative person

peasant poor person working in the countryside

pewter mixture of lead with tin or other metal

Pope head of the Catholic church. He lives in Rome.

population number of people in a country

Puritan deeply religious person with high standards of behaviour

range cooking fireplace

sanitation flushing toilets and drains

scabbard holder for keeping a sword in

sermon talk on a particular subject, usually given in church

subject person who must obey a monarch

tanner maker of leather from animal skins

tax money payments people make to those who govern them

virginal Tudor musical instrument like a harpsichord

wattle and daub twigs and sticks plastered with mud or clay

whey curds lumpy milk, like cottage cheese

yeoman well-to-do farmer with his own land

Index